modelrooms
space planner

A guide to interior layouts for selfbuilding, remodelling or extending

Katie Galvin
and
Modelrooms

Modelrooms Space Planner
A guide to interior layouts for selfbuilding, remodelling or extending

A modelrooms Book
Published and Distributed by Modelrooms Ltd
Unit 6
Sunshine Ind Est
Crumlin Rd
Dublin 12
Ireland
00 353 1 4539990
sales@modelrooms.com
www.modelrooms.com

ISBN 978-0-9555410-0-1

Acknowledgements
Thanks to Margaret and to Joe.

While every effort has been made to check the accuracy of the information contained in this book, the publisher accepts no responsibility for misstatements made in it or any consequences arising from it. We recommend using skilled professionals for all planning, structural, plumbing and electrical work.
Magnets not suitable for small children.
Warning:Magnets may have adverse affects on electronic equipment and other objects

Printed in Dublin by ColourBooks Ltd

contents

introduction

This book is intended to be a springboard for ideas. The plans are not intended to be taken as the best possible solution for the space but rather a suggestion of what the possibilities are. Feel free to use the blank plans to improve our ideas or better yet create your own house plan and play around with it until you have tried so many different options you are sure you have the best one. Some of our plans have deliberate flaws which we have pointed out because at modelrooms we believe when it comes to house building that 'learning from your mistakes' is really not the best way!

guide to modelrooms magnetic pieces

planning with modelrooms in 3 easy steps

One of the advantages of modelrooms is that it allows you to start planning almost immediately. The following steps allow you to get started quickly

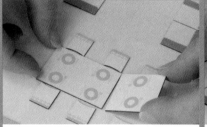

step 1:

Plan. The A5 white board will hold your magnets in place. Place it under your paper plans or draw your plans directly onto the white board with the dry wipe pen.
Alternatively use our blank plans in the book to get you started.

step 2:

Furnish. Try out different layouts using the magnetic scale furniture pieces.
Using a scissors and a scale rule to measure you can trim the magnets to create specific pieces of furniture. Remember that this is about a sence of space and how it fits your lifestyle rather than a technical drawing!

step 3:

Modify. Now for the fun part - Start dreaming and rearranging your house to reflect your ideal home. Keep an open mind - remember with modelrooms mistakes don't cost you anything!

modelrooms

Care of modelrooms: Board and pieces can be cleaned using a mild solution of washing up liquid and water with a soft cloth. Do not immerse product in water.

guide to modelrooms magnetic pieces

One of the strengths of modelrooms is the ease with which it allows you to **share ideas**.

Using a digital camera you can take a photo of your design and save, print or e-mail it. Carefully place on a photocopier or scanner to create a **copy** of your design.

The scale of the magnets provided is **1:50**, this means a metre is represented by 20 milimetres, however we have done the hard part so you can simply treat the scale rule on your modelroom as you would use a tape measure in your home.

Remember the **scale rule** will only work on the modelroom units and you need to use a regular tape measure for your real home dimensions.

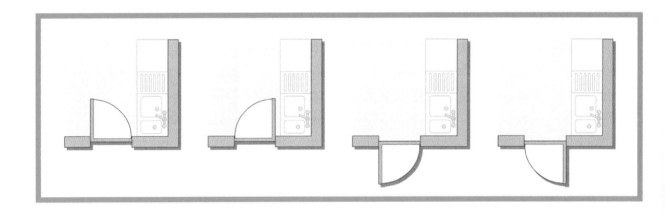

Our doors represent a standard **800mm door** without frame. Remember all doors have **four options** for hanging. Open to the left or right and into the room or out.

Make sure that furniture or kitchen units will **not obstruct** doors opening fully. The quarter circles represent the **swing arc** on a door and are used to best position your doors.

guide to circulation space

circulation space

The modelrooms people are designed to help you get the right **circulation** space between objects.
They each represent **600mm** (2 feet)d.

wheelchair accessability

Wheelchairs need **1500mm diameter** to turn around comfortably, as illustrated by our turning circle.
Motorised wheelchairs may need additional space.
A comfortable width for a wheelchair user is **900mm** which allows room for the chair and elbows.

In most situations a **circulation space** of between 600 and 700mm is recommended per person (our people are 600mm diameter), this represents a comfortable personal space.
Remember that this means that between two kitchen counters or a kitchen island unit and a counter to leave at least 1200mm, or enough room for **two people** to comfortably fit.
The figure of 600mm (2 feet) should be **increased** where you need to access something like a wardrobe door or to open drawers.
Corridor space should be 900mm (min).

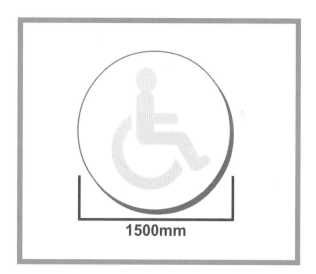

1500mm

kitchen ideas

When designing a kitchen one of the key success factors is how you position the cooker, fridge and sink. This is called creating the work triangle and getting these units as close together as possible to each other will make your kitchen more user friendly. It is not necessary for the items to literally be in a triangle.

The cooker and fridge should not be placed next to each other. Keep the work triangle away from busy doorways.

the value of a well designed kitchen is priceless

It is recommended to allow 1.2metres (4 feet) of circulation space where people are likely to pass each other. 700mm should also be used to allow people to pull a chair out from a table.

Check the plumbing implications of moving a sink. It is usually easier to leave the sink in the same place and simply fit a new one, but weigh up the advantages of a different location against the cost implications before making your decision.

One of the most common complaints in kitchens is lack of counter space, so try and get as much counter space as possible. Allow enough counter space to facilitate normal use such as food preparation, stacking dirty dishes, even somewhere to place the shopping bags while unpacking.

Think about storage in a logical fashion. Key things to watch out for are making sure there is room for pots and pans near the cooker, storage for dishes and cutlery near the dishwasher and near the food preparation area. As the kitchen is normally the busiest room in the house it is worth taking the time to plan it well.

large kitchen

Room shape	L
Length	7.6m
Width	4.2m
Square Metres	32m2
Square Feet	343 ft2

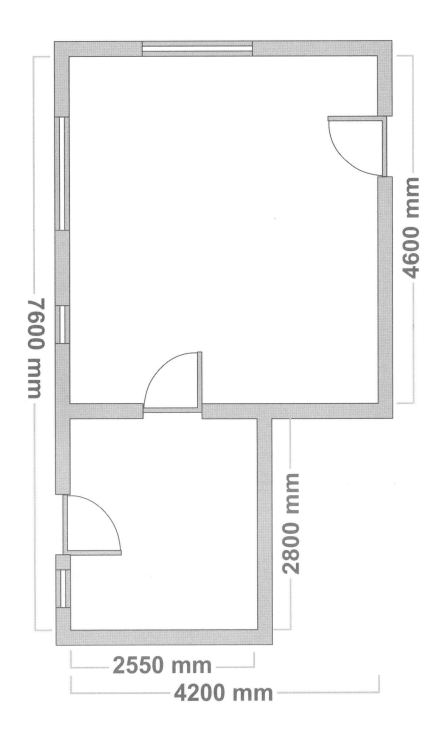

7600 mm

4600 mm

2800 mm

2550 mm

4200 mm

large kitchen

hints

The kitchen triangle does not literally mean a triangle – in this case they are all in a line but it works well as they are close to each other, which is the real objective of the kitchen triangle. If possible try to include the dishwasher nearby too.

tips

Rehanging the door between the kitchen and utility to open towards the sink avoids banging it off the fridge and gives more space to the kitchen.Conservation of heat in the kitchen is maximised by having the outside door open from the utility.

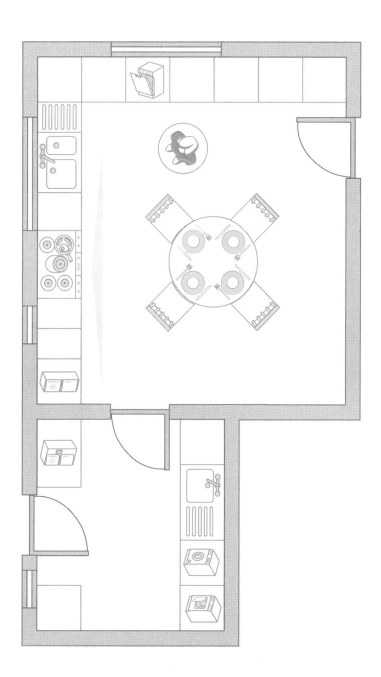

large kitchen

tips

The corner between the fridge and the sink is a potential dead space, if the fridge is above counter height. It may make more sense to move the fridge elsewhere.

hints

Taking away the utility wall creates a large light filled kitchen, with a compact working area and a great kitchen triangle.

The dining area can seat eight to ten people comfortably.

The introduction of two patio doors opens up the dining area to the garden, and adds extra light.

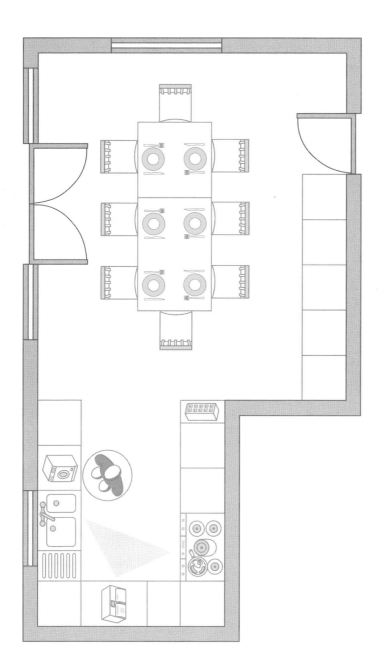

large kitchen

hints

Create a living area within the kitchen if space is limited elsewhere in the house. The open plan layout gives the impression of more space, and will also reduce the heating bills by combining the kitchen with the living areas.

tips

By opening the patio doors outward the space in the dining area of the kitchen is maximised.

The addition of two short walls between the kitchen and living areas allows the TV and coffee table to 'sit' more comfortably behind them.

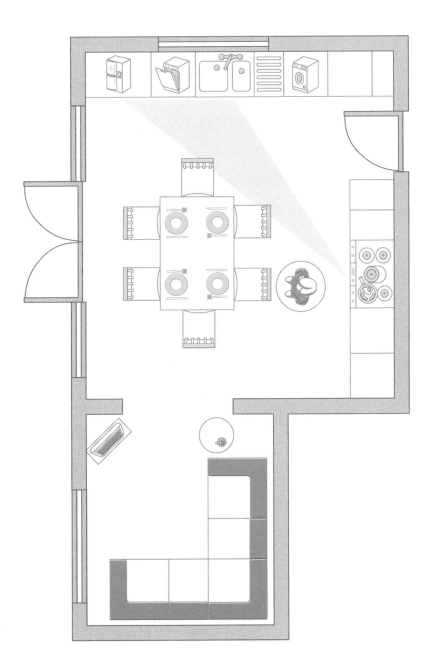

bathroom ideas

A thoughtfully designed bathroom is a wonderful addition to any room.

The bathroom is one of the most expensive rooms to change as a complete overhaul can require a plumber, electrician, tiller, painter, and possibly a builder. It makes sense to plan carefully to make sure you get exactly what you want and avoid expensive extra work. During design consider how much storage you will need. Given the small size of most bathrooms items like the linen basket or a bin can dramatically reduce the size of your space.

Prepare a checklist of what you would like to store in your bathroom before starting to design.

The bathroom tends to be one of the smallest rooms in the house and soft colours with subtle patterns will open the room up.

relax in your own sanctuary

Pale colours usually work best for bathrooms. If you are planning on selling your home a neutral colour scheme will appeal to a wider range of buyers.

With lighter colours you can easily change the colour of your room by introducing new items like coloured towels.

Before dramatically changing your layout it is a good idea to get advice from a professional on the costs and effort involved. You may find that moving fixed items like toilets or built in showers does not justify the costs involved.

16

small bathroom

plan

Room shape	rectangle
Length	2.8m
Width	2.1m
Square Metres	6m2
Square Feet	63 ft2

hints

Typical bathroom layout of newer homes. Practical design where the centre of the room is multifunctioning. The space at the end of the bath could be fitted with valuable storage space. In a case like this getting something made to fit will usually make the most efficent use of the space available

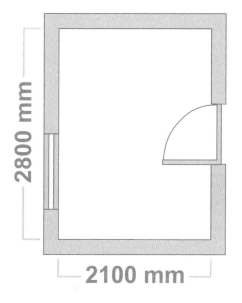

2800 mm

2100 mm

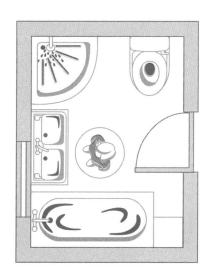

small bathroom

hints

Having a combined shower and bath is a great way to free up space in smaller bathrooms. The extra space created can be used for additional storage often underestimated when planning a bathroom.

tips

Bathroom fittings are all available as corner units. They are generally used when they suit the shape of a room best but can also be used to soften the shape of a bathroom. One or two corner units is the most that should be used in any bathroom.

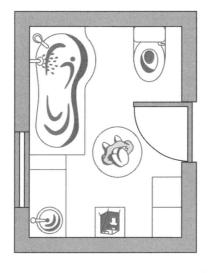

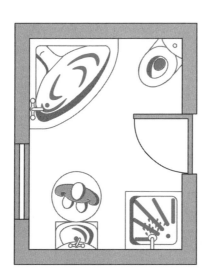

open plan extension

House Type	Older Terraced
Length	8m
Width	5.5m
Square Metres	44m2
Square Feet	473 ft2

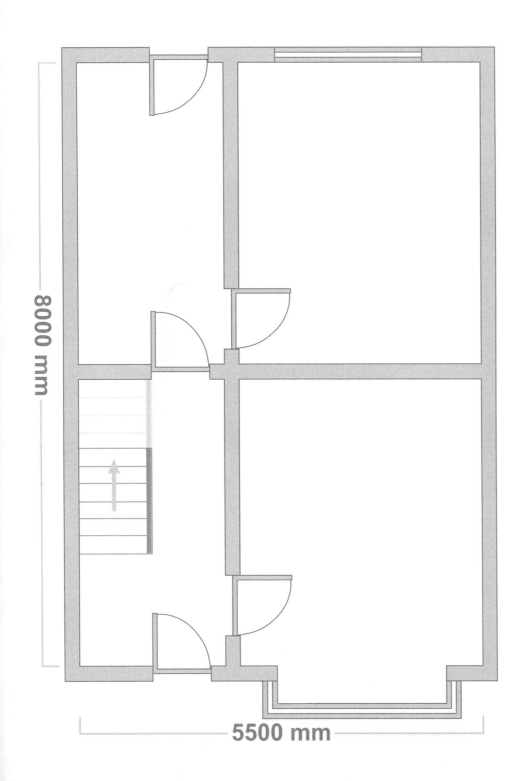

8000 mm

5500 mm

open plan extension

hints & tips

A typical older terraced house, where the kitchen left no room for modern appliances. The simplest solution to this is to knock the dividing wall between the kitchen and dining room to create space for the extra units in a modern kitchen. A half height wall behind the cooker would screen the kitchen while dining.

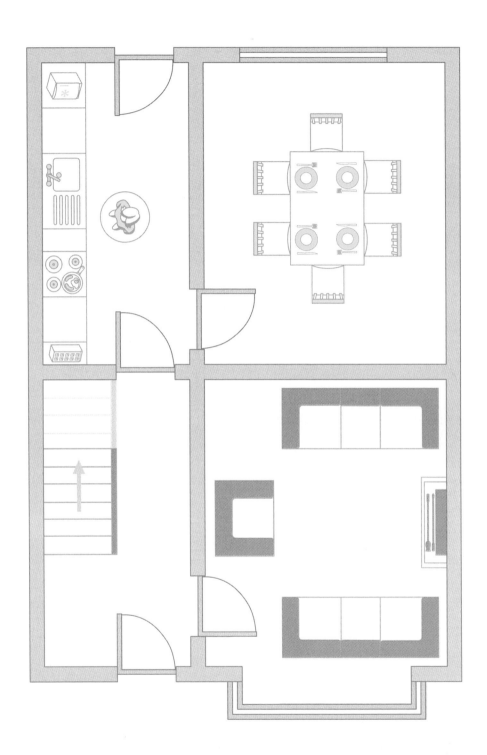

open plan extension

hints & tips

Extending into the garden will make a very smart sun filled living dining area. The open plan layout enhances the informal feel of the home. This room is now the hearth of the home with three distinct areas for relaxing, dining and cooking.

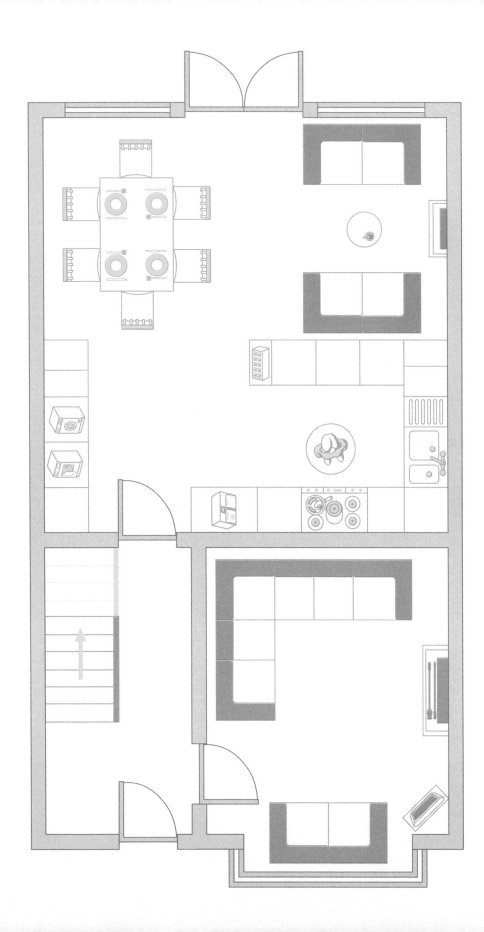

open plan extension

hints

If the rear of the house is North facing, consider an L shaped glazed extension. This could capture the evening sun in the living area.

tips

Simply swap the location of the dining table and the sofa if you prefer to eat with the evening sun, in this multifunctioning kitchen/living space.

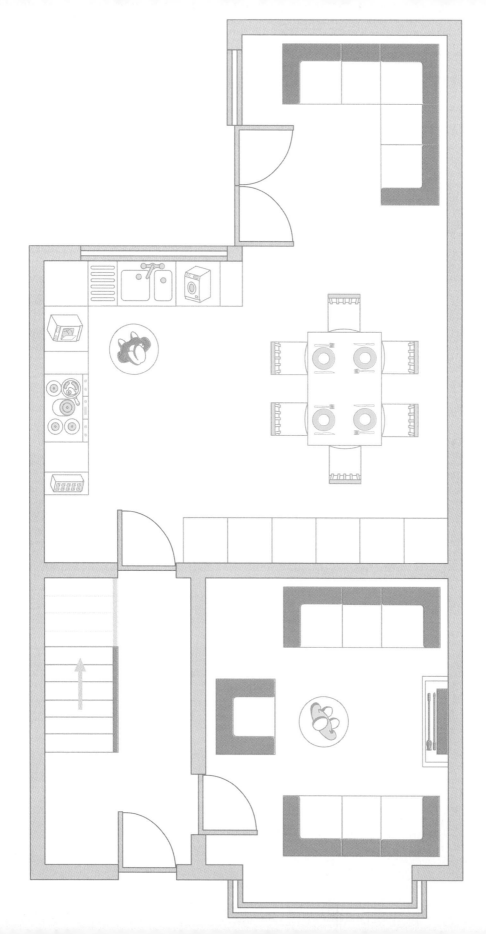

livingroom checklist

modelrooms	currently have	want to have	needs socket
sofa			
arm chairs			
sofa bed			
footstool			
side board			
coffee table			
fireplace			
bookshelves			
tv			
stereo			
speakers			
cd/dvd storage			
desk			
chairs			
computer			
games console			
kids toys			
wood / coal storage			
lamps			
standard lamp			
piano			
display cabinet			
plants			

living room

31

Room shape	Rectangle
Length	7.6m
Width	4.8m
Square Metres	36m2
Square Feet	393ft2

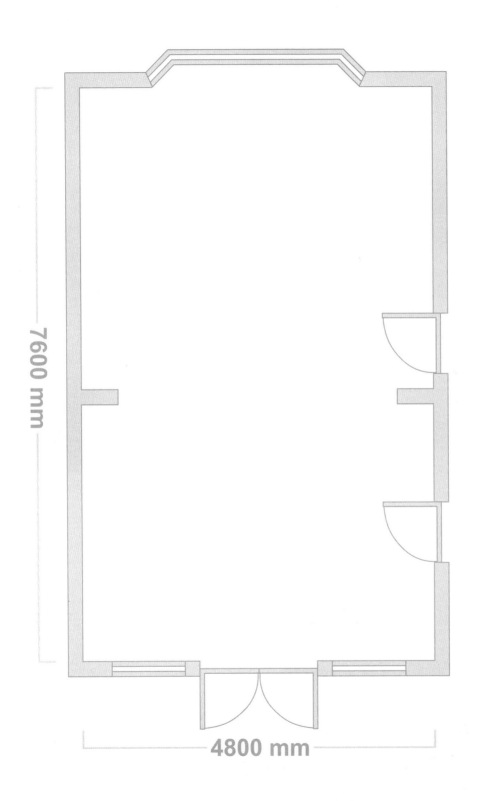

7600 mm

4800 mm

living room

hints & tips

The logical place for the dining room is adjacent to the kitchen but it is not necessary to be bound by the rules. If sunlight is better at the back of the house and you love your garden, why not break with tradition and reverse the living and dining room.

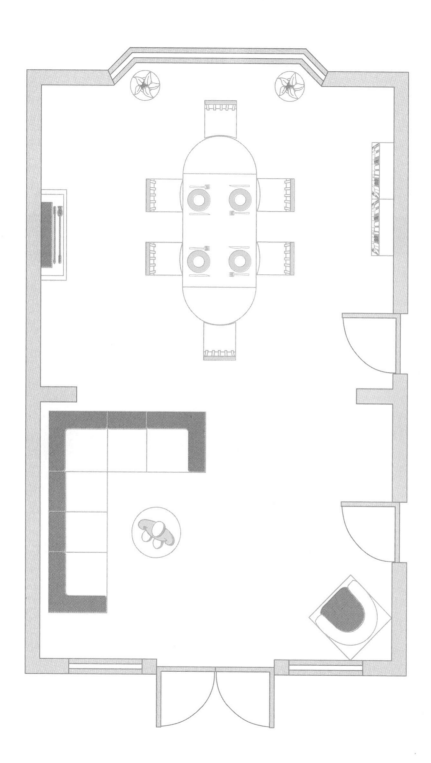

living room

hints

Many older houses have formal dining rooms that are rarely used. If this is the case consider putting it to full time use as a music room or simply as an extended living space.

tips

If you are putting your house on the market at a later stage, try to revert back to the dining room, as a conventional layout will normally appeal to a much wider market.

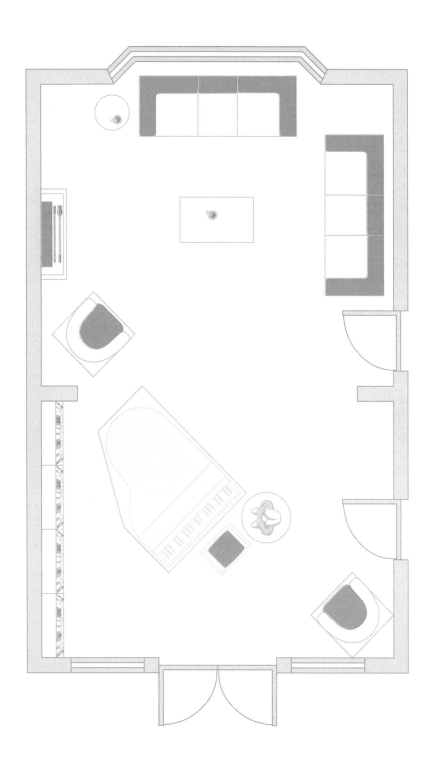

bathroom checklist

model rooms	currently have	want to have	notes
bath			
shower			
showerbath			
sink			
double sink			
toilet			
bidet			
wetroom			
hot press			
towel rail			
heated towel rail			
bathroom cabinets			
mirror			
laundry basket			
cleaning products			
spare toilet rolls			
toiletries			
cosmetics			
candles &oil burner			
kids bath toys			
weighing scales			
spare towels			
bath mat			

family bathroom

plan

Room shape	rectangle
Length	3m
Width	2.6m
Square Metres	8m2
Square feet	84 ft2

hints

This plan opens up the bathroom to create a spacious luxurious room. Opening the door against the wall would maximise the space. The room is large enough to accommodate an extra large shower and full size bath. Alternatively it could fit a much larger bath or shower easily enough.

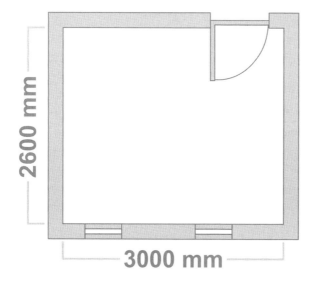

2600 mm

3000 mm

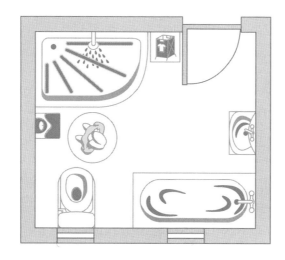

family bathroom

hints

For the second bathroom in the house consider investing in the luxury of a sauna or steam room. Having a small window in the shower area is feasible but would not be the ideal scenario. When faced with an awkward shape look beyond the conventional for something such as a corner toilet which works great here.

tips

If a large bathroom is adjacent to a bedroom consider the possibility of splitting the bathroom and gaining an en suite. This works perfectly when the original bathroom can still accommodate a bath, as in this case. Otherwise it may be possible to extend into the bedroom a little to achieve the en suite, without losing the original bath

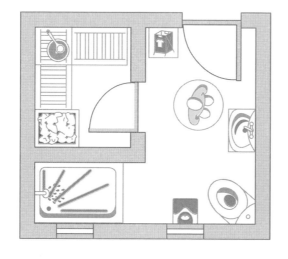

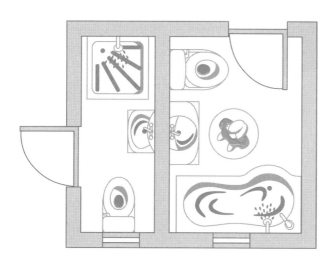

big ideas for small spaces

simplicity creates space

Its always a great challenge making more out of something small. Also allow as much circulation space as possible by the door to give a first impression of space.

Place a large mirror opposite or adjacent to the window which will bounce more light into the room. Streamline your window with blinds rather than curtains.

Choose compact furniture for the room and place it as neatly as possible. Furniture with legs rather than solid pieces will give the illusion of more floor space

In a room horizontal stripes will give a sense of width to the room and using long shelves or a couple of painted stripes will give the appearance of length.

Use built in shelving or wall cupboards to free up floor space rather than freestanding units. Keep the flooring neutral and try not to break it up with rugs.

44

one bed artisan cottage

45

House Type	One Bed Artisan
Length	5.8m
Width	3.8m
Square Metres	22m2
Square Feet	237 ft2

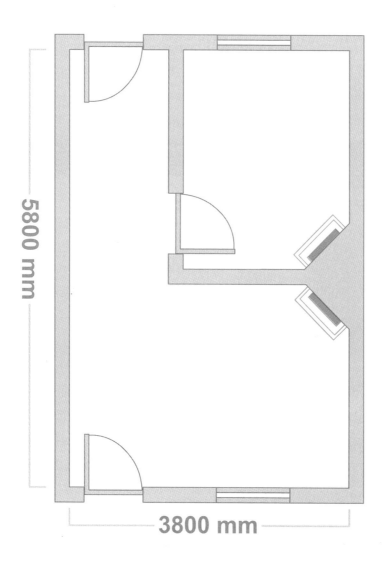

5800 mm

3800 mm

one bed artisan cottage

hints

An original one bed Artisan Cottage with no facilities for modern day living. The one bedroom can barely fit a double bed, and the original house had no indoor bathroom in it. The bedroom is an akward shape and quite small for a double bed and sufficient storage. The corner fireplaces in the living and bedroom make for a quirky feature but with the limited space available are not very practical.

It is almost impossible to modernise this house without extending and remodelling.

tips

Sometimes an extension involves remodelling an existing floorplan for the optimum layout. This bedroom and bathroom are built around a small internal courtyard which throws light and fresh air through the house.

The glass door to the courtyard retains the light at the dining end. Use of underfloor heating, instead of traditional wall mounted radiators, is a great way of creating more useable space when every bit counts. A good way of dividing the space up visually, is through the use of a clever lighting plan where the dining and living areas are softer.

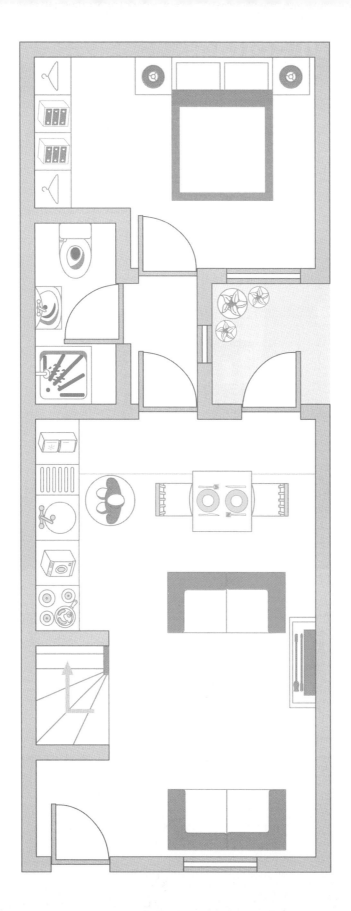

one bed artisan cottage

hints

Many smaller artisan dwellings do not have sufficient headroom in the attic for a habitable room conversion.

A mezzanine is one alternative, in this case it has been used to create a gallery style study with lots of storage.

tips

Adding rooflights would make this area brighter, with the bonus of adding extra natural light to the ground floor.

A glass panelled balustrade to the mezzanine gives it the wow factor.

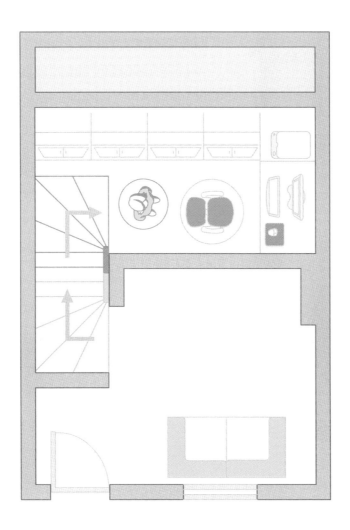

green living

There are many ways to incorporate green living into your design.

Try to us natural materials in the home where possible, such as wood, linoleum, cork, Hessian and organic paint. They usually cost more but health is wealth!

Fit a water filter where required to prolong the life of some appliances. A dual flush toilet system will reduce water wastage.

Consider the energy rating on electrical appliances before buying and fit energy saving light bulbs. Save money by including good insulation in your home. Insulating the water tank will ensures the heat is not lost and using timer devices on the heating system will also improve their efficiency greatly.

When planning a new kitchen layout try to facilitate storage for recycling. Consider using a pull out bin unit with different compartments for glass, paper, plastic, cans, and organic waste.

save the planet while you save money

53

House Type	Bungalow
Length	11.5m
Width	8m
Square Metres	92m2
Square Feet	990 ft2

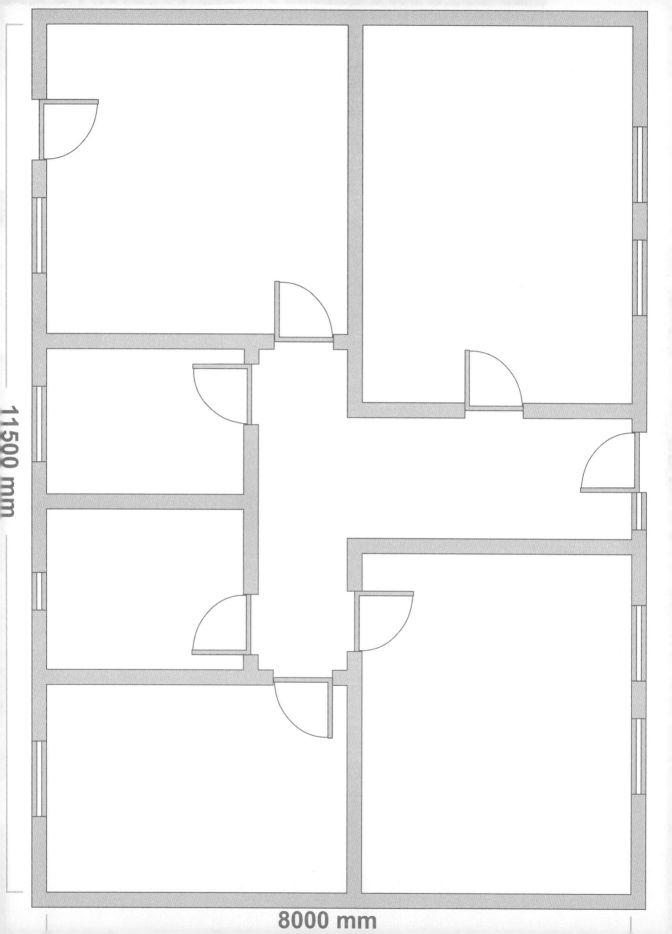

11500 mm

8000 mm

bungalow with attic conversion

hints

Perfectly proportioned three bed bungalow with a generous entrance hall, It has good wheelchair accessability throughout. The simplicity of this design is its strength.

tips

There are separate living and kitchen areas. Only one door into the living room ensures a very peaceful space.

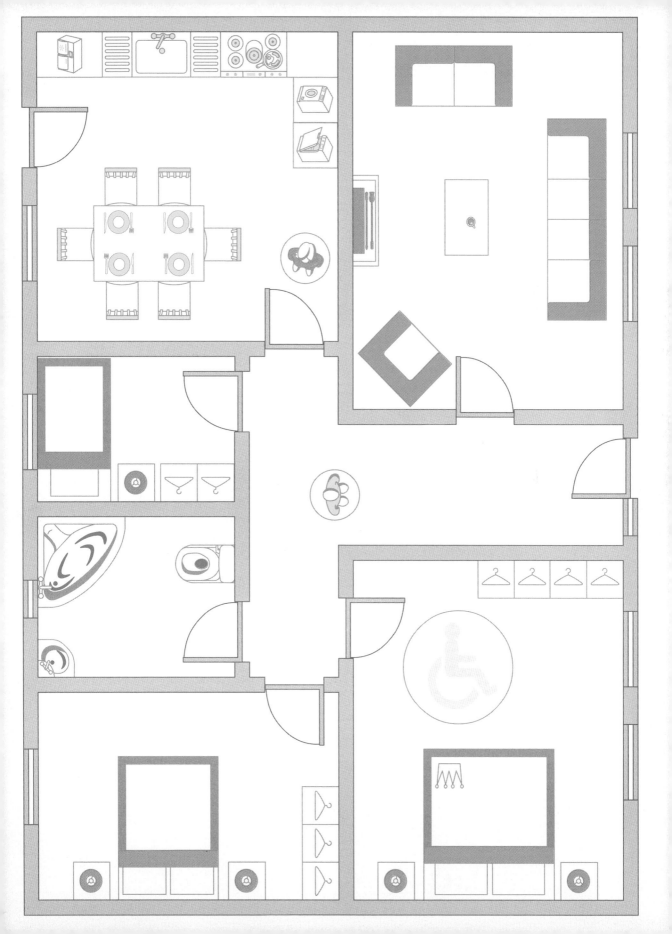

bungalow with attic conversion

hints

With the minimum disruption the attic can be converted in this house. The house now has four double bedrooms with one of them being a luxury en-suite master bedroom. The old single bedroom not only accommodates the stairs but a small home office space or storage area underneath. The spiral stairs could alternatively be replaced with a regular stairs if preferred. There may be limited furniture access with a spiral.

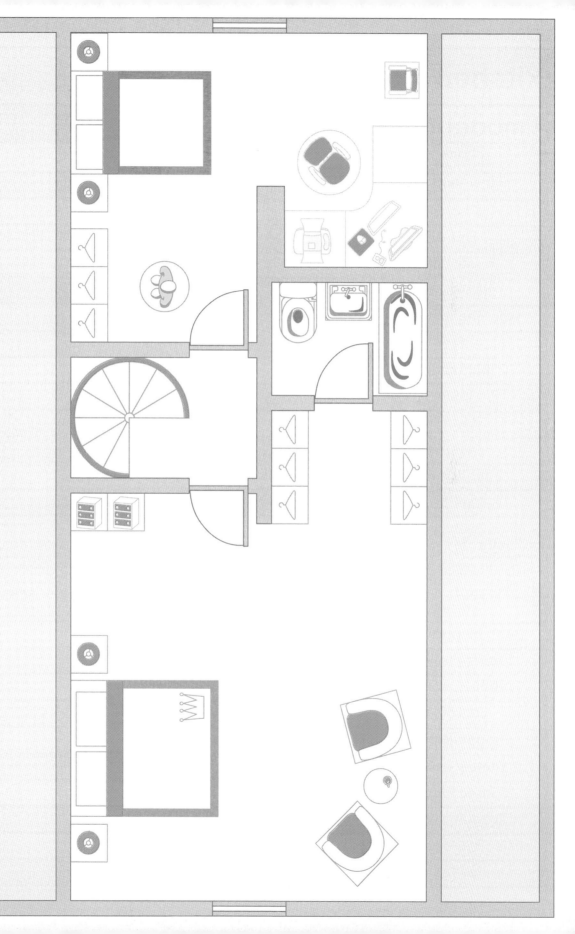

kitchen checklist 1 of 2

model rooms	currently have	want to have	needs socket
sink			
oven			
hob			
fridge			
freezer			
dishwasher			
washing machine			
dryer			
microwave			
table			
chairs			
dresser			
highchair			
kettle			
toaster			
sandwich toaster			
griller machine			
juicer			
blender			
coffee maker			
kitchen scales			
bread bin			
chopping board			
utensil holder			
knife block			
biscuit barrel			
tea/coffee/sugar jars			
tea/coffee pot			

modelrooms	currently have	want to have	needs socket
fruit bowl			
veg rack			
spice rack			
wine rack			
pots & pans			
baking trays etc.			
cook books			
cook book holder			
tv			
stereo			
cd's			
computer			
kids toys			
ironing board			
sweeping brush			
rubbish/ recycling bin			
cleaning products			
laundry basket			
vacuum cleaner			
pet baskets			
litter tray			
notice board			
towels			
table linen			

rectangular kitchen

Room shape	Rectangle
Length	6.5m
Width	4.3m
Square Metres	28m2
Square Feet	300 ft2

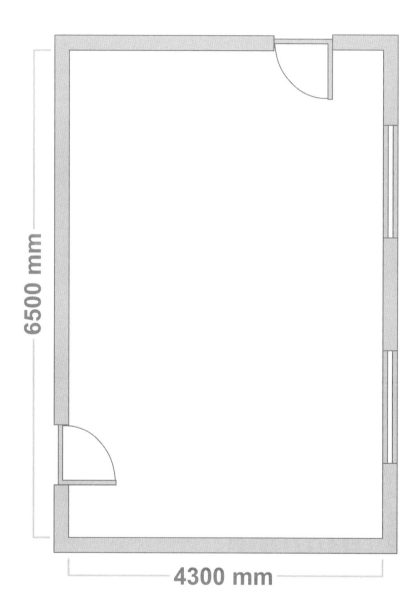

6500 mm

4300 mm

rectangular kitchen

63

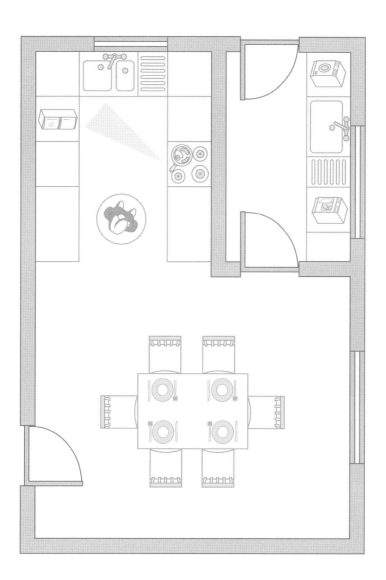

rectangular kitchen

hints & tips

Create an open plan kitchen/dining/livingroom by removing the utility walls. This would require careful planning with overhead units to compensate for the loss of storage in the utility. Storage is one of the most important things to consider in the kitchen. A round table suits the new layout of the kitchen, and can seat four to six easily.

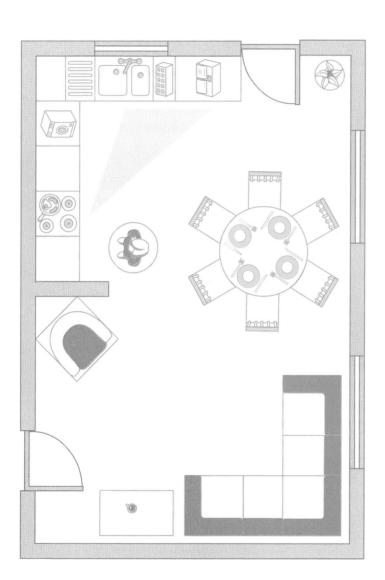

rectangular kitchen

hints & tips

Remember to allow 1200mm (4 ft) of circulation space between the island unit and kitchen counters so that someone can work comfortably at the same time at each.

hints & tips

The open plan layout delights anyone who views their kitchen as a communal area for entertaining family and friends. An island unit with a cooker is perfect for preparing food as you chat to your guests, but be sure to choose a quiet extractor fan for overhead, and ensure the lighting is sufficient.

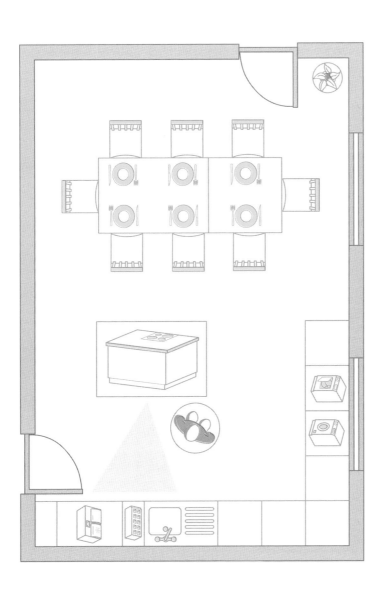

creating personality in your home

The secret to creating a unique sense of personality in your space is in carefully choosing your accessories. Don't leave selecting these until your job is done. Plan ahead.

When you have selected a few key items to hold onto, use them to springboard ideas or a theme for the décor. A whole room can be built around a single painting or sculpture.

An old antique may have looked dated on a crowded dresser, but put it on its own in an alcove with a spotlight or coloured background and you get a great mix of old and new to liven up any room.

If you can not decide what to focus on then try a process of elimination. Collect all of the things you are considering and remove one or two each day for a week until you are left with the items that really work for you.

If you have some key items you still love after all these years then aim to enhance them and give them a new lease of life.

accessories create the personality in a room

garage conversion

hints & tips

This is a standard 1970s family home, with a very large kitchen cum breakfast room and separate utility. The combined living dining area with windows at opposite ends ensures the room gets the maximum sunlight. An integrated garage can be used for your car, as a workshop, or simply for storage.

scale 1:100

garage conversion

hints

The house has been updated by converting the garage to a playroom / games room. By remodelling the cloakroom the games room can be accessed from the hall.

tips

The utility and kitchen are combined to make one large informal living dining area. The kitchen and garden merge together when you throw open the patio doors.

garage conversion

scale 1:100

bedroom checklist

modelrooms	currently have	want to have	needs socket
superking size bed			
king size bed			
double bed			
single bed			
bunk beds			
childs bed			
cot			
bedside lockers			
wardrobes			
walk in wardrobe			
en-suite			
dresser			
desk			
chair/s			
mirror			
lamps			
blanket box			
shoe rack			
tv/stereo			
clothes/shoes			
accessories			
toiletries			
bed linen			

Room shape	Rectangle
Length	5.5m
Width	3.4m
Square Metres	19m2
Square Feet	201 ft2

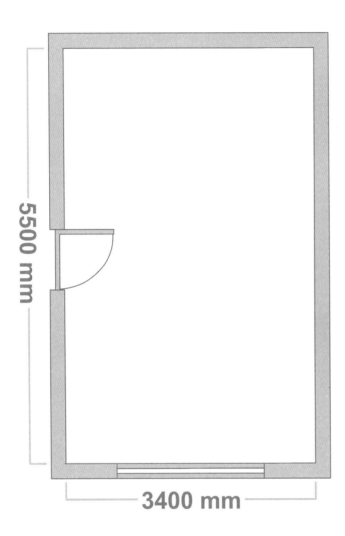

5500 mm

3400 mm

bedroom en-suite

hints & tips

This is a spacious bedroom with ample storage and a generous en-suite shower room. The dead space beside this shower would be ideal for recessed, tiled shelving within the shower. In the master bedroom it is important to provide adequate stotage for clothes, shoes, and accessories. Clutter in this room is one of the most frequently heard complaints. If possible allow enough room for a relaxing space so the room can provide a peacefull sanctuary from the rest of the house occasionally. Having different types of lighting changes the mood.

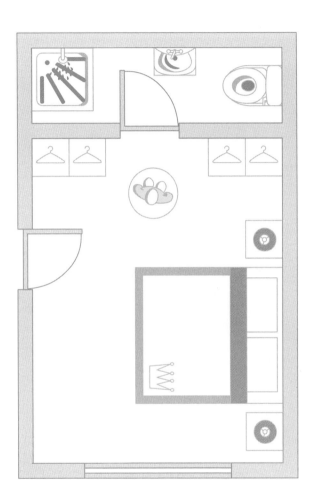

bedroom en-suite

hints
This layout not only gives the luxury of a walk in wardrobe but also an uncluttered look to the sleeping area of the room. The en-suite entrance is now out of view.

tips
For small bathrooms put storage cupboards on the wall to save space. The sink and toilet can also be wall mounted to give added floor space back to the bathroom.

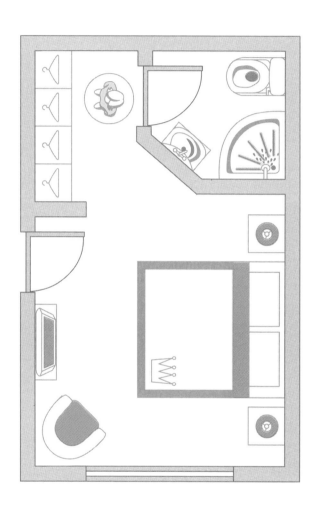

adding value to your home

We all have ideas on improvements we would like to make to our homes to improve them but some ideas are better than others at adding value to your home.

In general if you are making changes the rule is 'keep it simple' and stick with tried and trusted improvements.

selling or staying, adding value is always a good idea

Expect a good kitchen adding up to 15% to the resale value of your home. Next in line is the bathroom which can add significantly to the value of your house. Don't be misled by the small size of this room as it is usually an expensive investment.

Upgrading the central heating will create a very positive impression with potential buyers as a good heating system is always a great selling feature.

Adding an en-suite bathroom is another good improvement but make sure it is not at the cost of another room as an additional bedroom will be worth more than an extra bathroom normally.

A good garden will always add value to your home. At the very least the garden should be well maintained, and its always worth investing in flowering plants to brighten it up.

remodelled terrace

House	Terraced downstairs
Length	9.5m
Width	3.8m
Square Metres	36m2
Square Feet	388 ft2

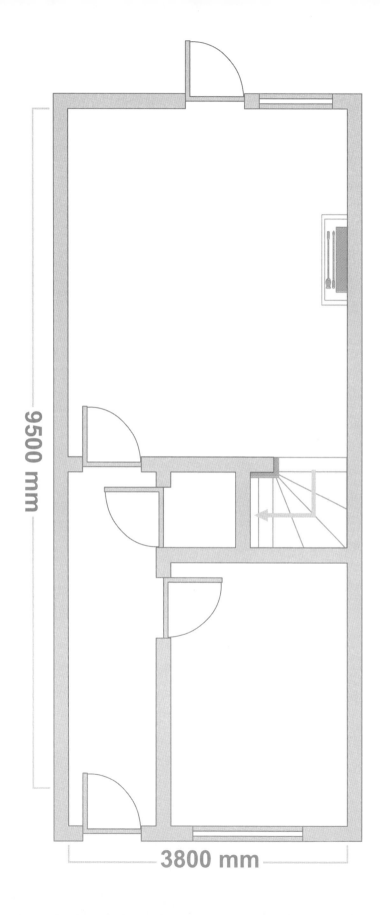

9500 mm

3800 mm

remodelled terrace

hints

This layout is designed for the lounge to be the main social area of the house, with a small functioning kitchen. A narrow hallway such as this provides little room for furniture. With clever use of wall mounted coat racks, shelving and mirrors, it can still function as more than an area to pass through. Since it creates a first impression to your house it is worth giving thought to the design of the hall. It also acts as a link between the kitchen and living room, it is important that it works in harmony with both of these rooms.

Use of mirrors and white or pale coloured walls in smaller rooms will create more light.

tips

Create space in small kitchens by putting shelves over counters for everyday storage, and ceiling height cupboards for seldom used items.

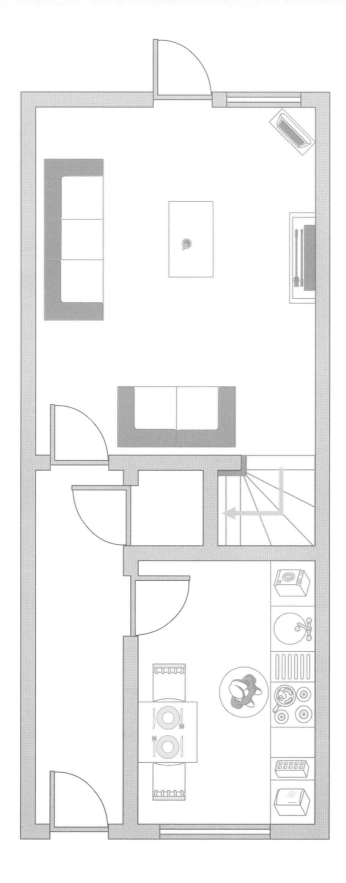

remodelled terrace

hints & tips

A downstairs cloakroom adds value to any size home. Adding the hall space to the living room increases the useable space, although at the cost of some privacy. Make the most of the small space in the kitchen by putting built in seating with storage beneath it. The structural implications of this remodelled home are quite significant.

89

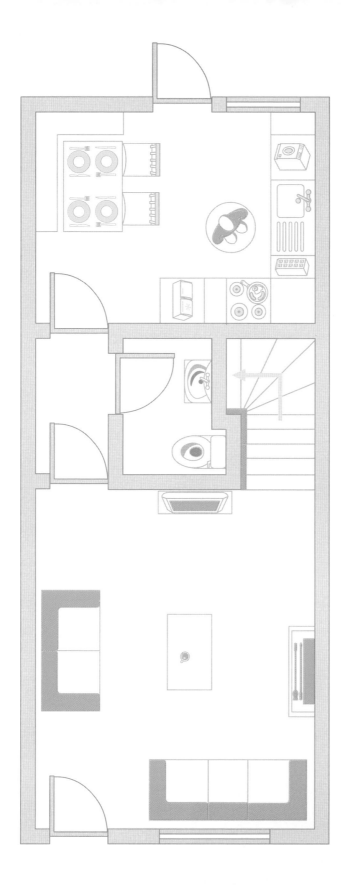

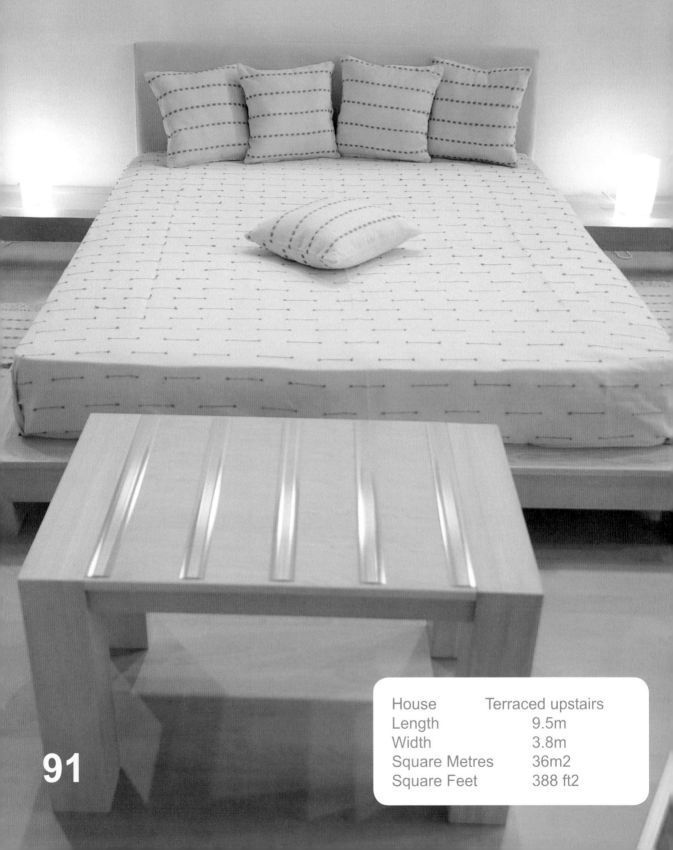

remodelled terrace

91

House	Terraced upstairs
Length	9.5m
Width	3.8m
Square Metres	36m2
Square Feet	388 ft2

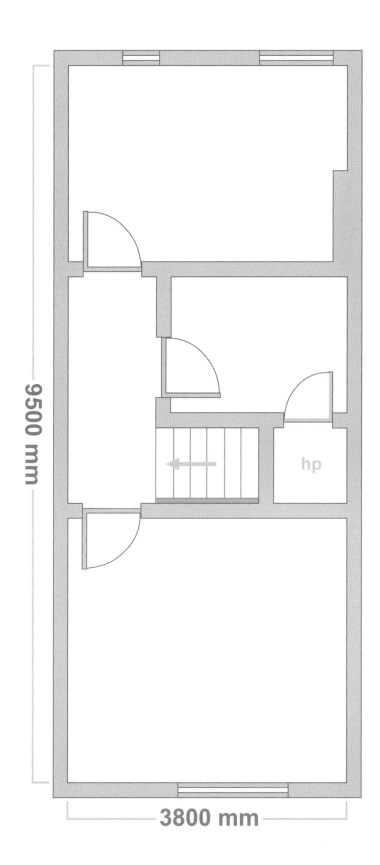

9500 mm

3800 mm

hp

remodelled terrace

hints & tips

Typical bedroom layout of a small house with two well proportioned light filled bedrooms, and a good sized bathroom. A 'd' shaped bath gives more showering space.

Having the airing cupboard in the bathroom where space allows gives the added luxury of warm dry towels.

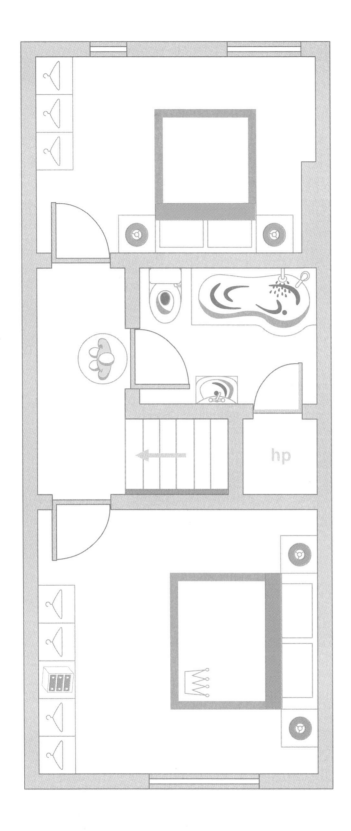

hp

remodelled terrace

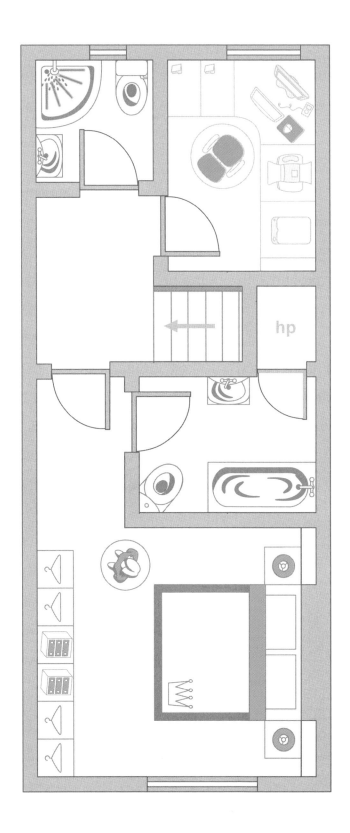

hp

pre planning

Before starting to invest in improvements to your home it is always worth doing some preparation.

Set your objectives for the project and why you are building or extending. Typical objectives include creating more space, increasing the value of the property or making better use of existing space.

Decide on your budget up front. This budget should be broken down into the different parts like planning, design, building and decorating.

Break down expenditures on fixtures, fittings, materials, labour costs and professional fees.

Decide on your planning, building and finishing timescales. Often improvements are driven by a date like wanting to have the project complete before Christmas or a big event like the birth of a child.

Look around you for inspiration on the improvements you would like to make. Review plans of homes you like from magazines, friends homes, or create new designs with modelrooms.

Consider your lifestyle habits. Identify how much of your time you spend working from home, entertaining guests, watching television, listening to music, cooking etc. This will help you decide where you should plan your improvements.

a good plan creates a strong foundation

kitchen extension

House Type	Townhouse
Length	6.7m
Width	4.8m
Square Metres	32m2
Square Feet	346 ft2

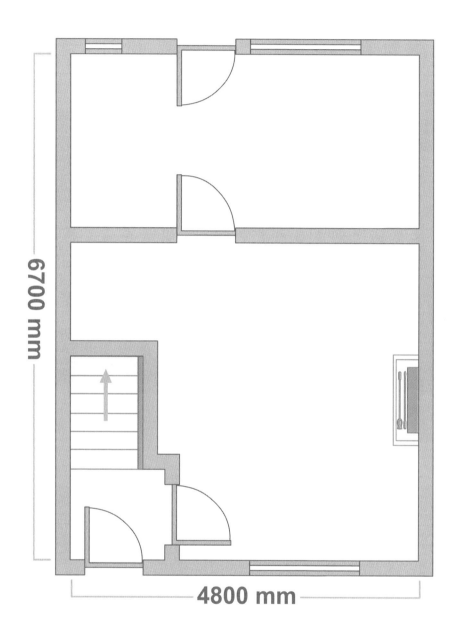

6700 mm

4800 mm

kitchen extension

hints
Open up the space under the stairs (usually filled with clutter) and you now have a compact home office.

tips
The proportions of a room are more important than the square area. Choose whether to prioritise your kitchen or living room where space is limited and make that room the main focal point of the house.

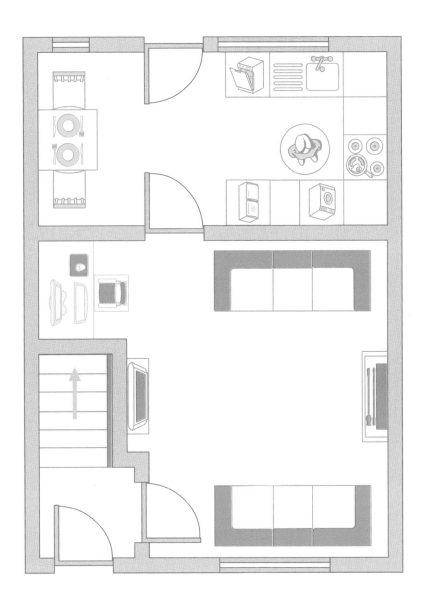

kitchen extension

hints & tips

This extension spans the back of the house to create a large dining kitchen, with utility and cloakroom off the lobby. The toilet should not open directly off the kitchen. Extra windows and glass patio doors maximise the natural light throughout the whole room. Choose soft lighting for the dining area and stronger lighting elswhere.

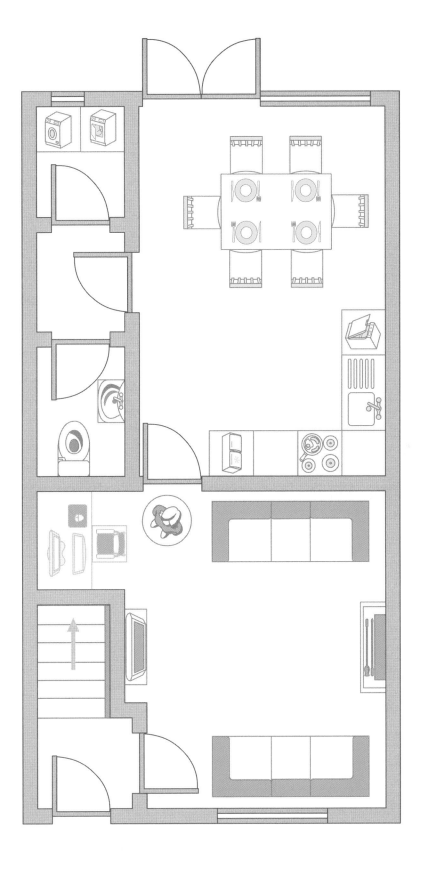

colour

Rather than painting the wall with a test colour, use a sheet of paper, and move it around each wall to see how it looks with different amounts of light.

Check the colour at several times of the day, but paying particular attention to the time of day the room is mainly used.

Before choosing a colour scheme for a room it is a good idea to check the direction it faces. South facing rooms get the most sunlight and can take a cooler scheme of colours such as greens, blues, and whites.

North facing rooms will have a cooler outlook and you may want to balance this with warmer colours such as yellows, oranges, reds pinks and creams.

soft and floaty, dramatic or vibrant, your choice

large bathroom

plans

Room shape	rectangle
Length	3.7m
Width	3.3m
Square Metres	12m2
Square Feet	131 ft2

tips

Big family bathroom with bath, large shower, double sink, toilet, bidet and huge storage capacity. Hanging the door from the other side gives a better sense of privacy to the toilet area. In recent years a great bathroom has become almost as big a selling feature as the kitchen is.

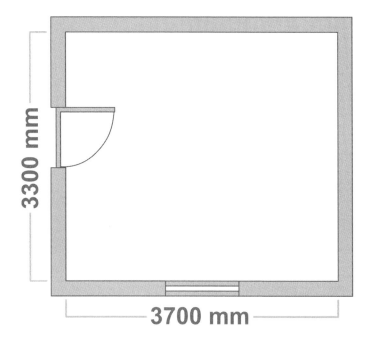

3300 mm

3700 mm

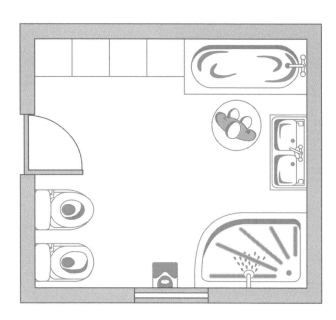

large bathroom

hints

A large walk in wardrobe or storage space can be accommodated here by remodelling this bathroom.

A built in sink storage unit makes the most of the available space.

When remodelling the bathroom the most difficult and expensive item to move is the toilet. They are normally situated by the outside wall for easier plumbing, though they do not have to be. The bathroom is also the one room in the house that does not need to have a window.

tips

The ultimate indulgence – converting one of the rooms in a period house, to a spacious bathroom, while retaining the original features, like fireplace and window, and all with the luxury of modern convenience.

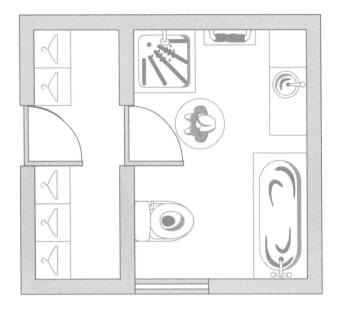

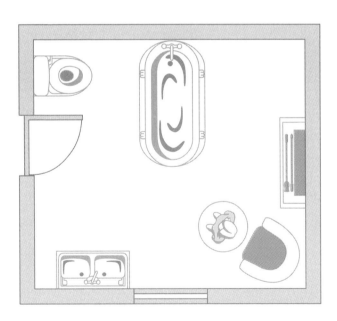

making the most of your space

The key to good design is understanding what you want from your space.

Consider your lifestyle when laying out your rooms. For example if you regularly entertain guests you will need dining space. If you have kids or plan on starting a family you will need play areas and to ensure that your home is child friendly.

Check that your room has enough space for people to circulate and experiment with different furniture layouts to make movement easier.

Look at how much natural light you have in your room. For example simply changing the wall colour can make a room brighter.

Consider whether you like your space to feel light and airy as lighter colours will give a greater feeling of space.

The best design is the one that works for your lifestyle

Darker colours will reduce the sense of space in a room.

How much storage do you need? Make a list of what exactly needs to be in the room or use a modelrooms checklist.

112

two bed artisan cottage

113

House Type	Artisan Cottage
Length	6m
Width	5.3m
Square Metres	32m2
Square Feet	342 ft2

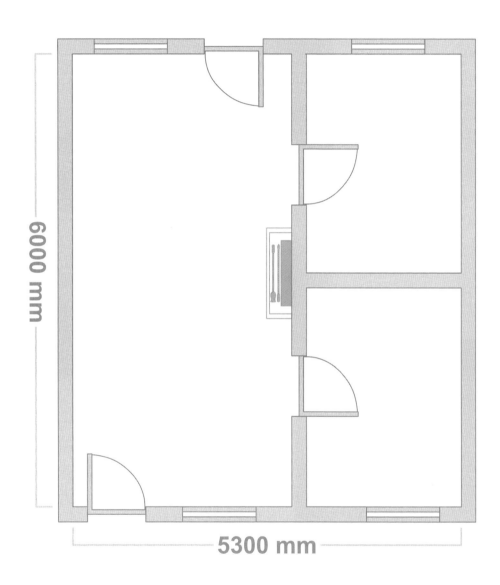

6000 mm

5300 mm

two bed artisan cottage

hints

This is a typical original artisan cottage with no modern facilities and two single bedrooms.

The biggest challenge here is remodelling around the chimney breast which runs through the centre of the floor plan. The lack of a bathroom makes renovation a must. The front elevation is retained but the interior is redesigned for a modern lifestyle. In small spaces providing adequate storage in the plan is essential. Generally, built in units make better use of the space.

tips

Normally turning a two bed house into a one bed house would devalue the property, but a one bed house with a bathroom is more valuable than a two bed with none.

This is particularly true if the new bedroom is a double with adequate storage, as in this case.

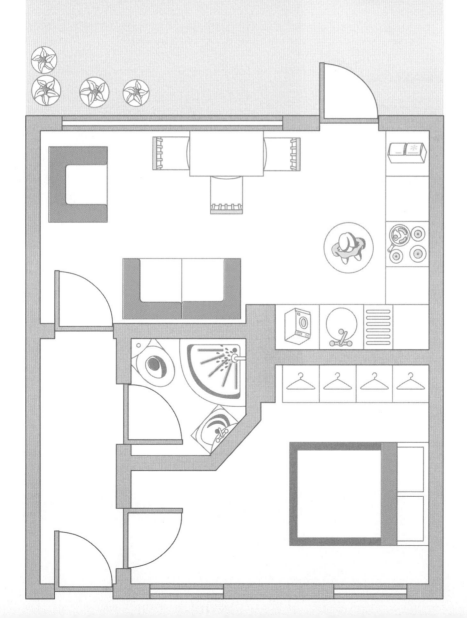

two bed artisan cottage

hints
Clearly defined kitchen, dining, and living areas in an L shaped room. A small computer desk fits perfectly into the fireplace niche. The working kitchen is tucked neatly away from the living area for added relaxation.

tips
The living area here would benefit from the addition of a roof light, and floor to ceiling window with a glass door, to maximise the available light. Whitening the patio walls would throw more light into the extension.

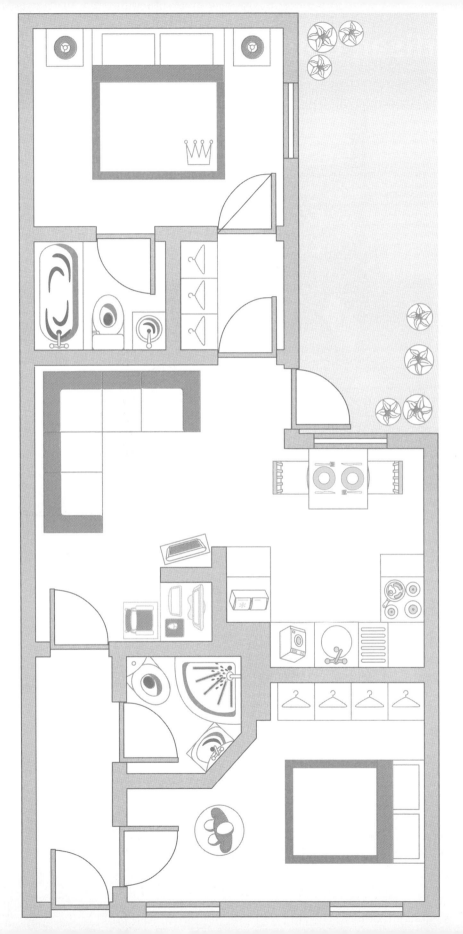

two bed artisan cottage

tips

The bedroom is well placed adjacent to the bathroom. A working home office, benefits from a large picture window overlooking the decked area if the home office is in constant use.

hints

The original fireplace is retained as the focal point of this large living space. An extension gives scope for the original house to be opened up as one big living room. A circular table with chairs fitting snugly under it suits this square shaped area. An internal courtyard with glass walls would fill the house with light.

119

two bed artisan cottage

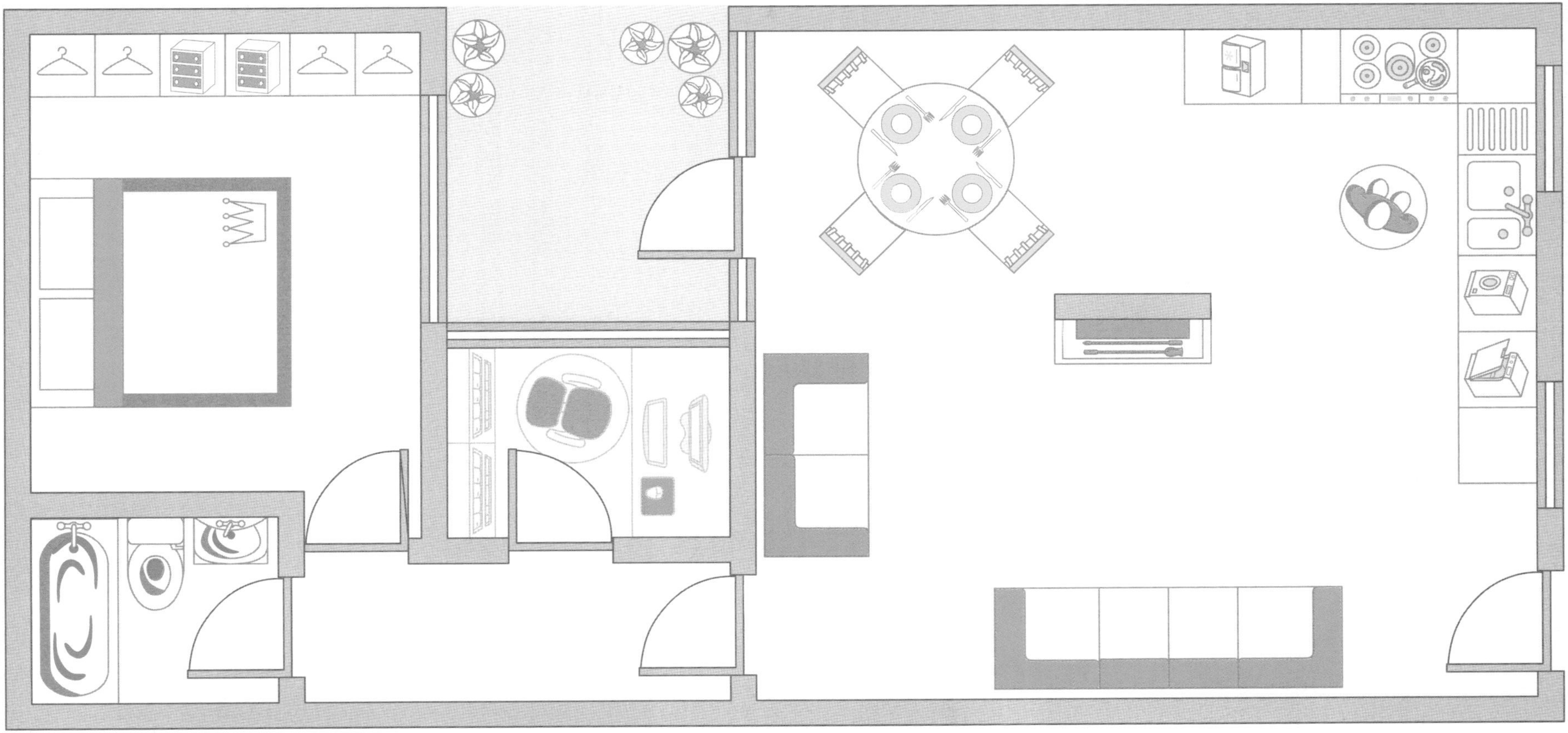

lighting

There are many creative ways of getting the most of your lighting and dramatically improving the ambience in your home.

Match your colour scheme with your choice of lighting. Light coloured surfaces reflect light and so need less light whereas dark wood and fabric tend to soak up the light and need more light to compensate.

Ensure your light switches are well positioned. Who hasn't had the experience of entering a dark room and fumbling for a light switch. The normal position for the switch is just inside the door at shoulder height. If the room has more than one door there should be a switch by each.

Create a feeling of warmth with mood lighting and don't forget the unique atmosphere created by candles. They really do create a great mood for parties, romantic dinners, or just chilling out.

Consider the natural light of a room. This will be determined by the orientation of a room combined with the size of your windows.

Use light from more than one direction to create a more interesting feeling in your room. Vertical and horizontal lighting will create a more rounded distribution.

lighting is the secret to successful interiors

L shaped kitchen

123

Room shape	L
Length	5.5m
Width	5.5m
Square Metres	22m2
Square Feet	238 ft2

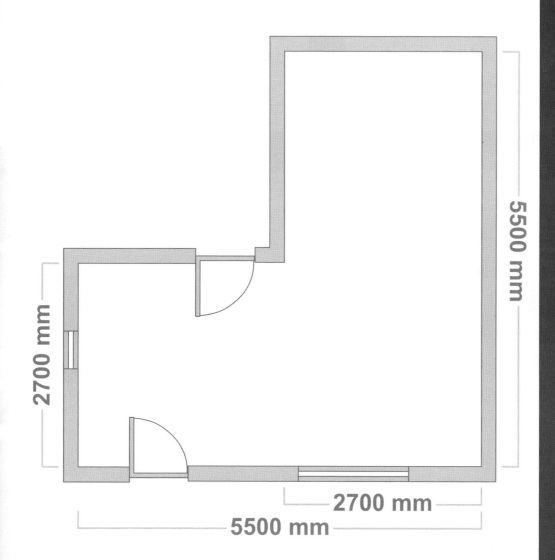

2700 mm

5500 mm

2700 mm

5500 mm

L shaped kitchen

hints

The dining area here can seat eight to ten people comfortably. The working kitchen is well situated nearby but provides inadequate counter space around the cooker and sink for the dining needs.

tips

Moving the fridge to the laundry end of the kitchen could be the solution, though It is not ideal to have the kitchen triangle cross between two doors. Counter space here is minimal and may not suit all.

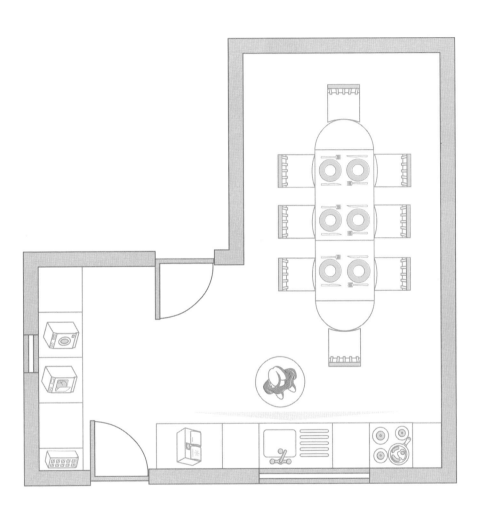

L shaped kitchen

hints

This kitchen has the added feature of a laundry room. This takes away the noisy washing machine and dryer with the added bonus of removing the laundry basket and its associated clutter. It would need to be well ventilated but does not necessarily need a window.

tips

Opening up two patio doors gives a sense of the outdoors while dining.

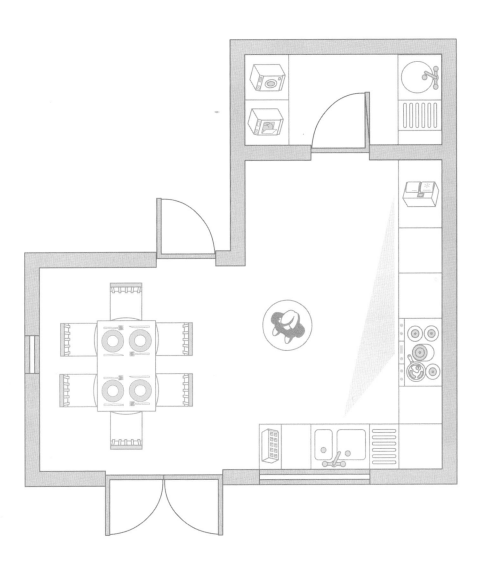

L shaped kitchen

The two arm chairs are well positioned to admire the garden without viewing the working kitchen. Glass patio doors add to the natural light

tips
A kitchen with a very efficient work triangle, and adequate circulation space. The dining area is well situated to be the central hub of the room.

129

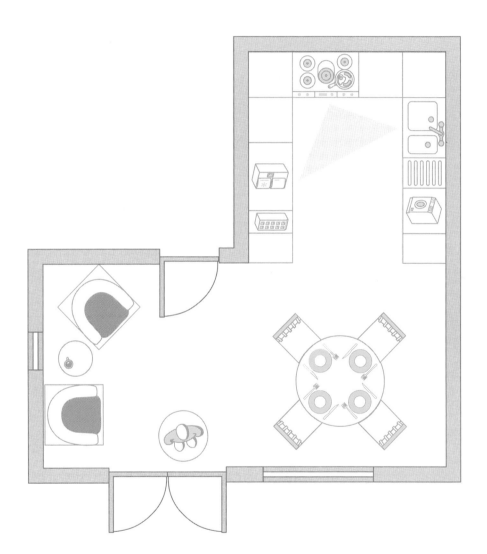

working with scales

identifying your drawing scale		◧model rooms
scale	1 metre equals	800 mm door equals
1:100	10 mm	8 mm
1:50	20 mm	16 mm
1:33	30 mm	24 mm
1:25	40 mm	32 mm
1:20	50 mm	40 mm
1:10	100 mm	80 mm
1:1	1000 mm	800 mm

A handy way to quickly check the scale of a drawing is to measure an internal door. The typical measurement for these is 800mm. This is by not foolproof but acts as a rough reference only.

changing scale on a photocopier ◧model rooms

change from	to 1:25	to 1:33	to 1:50	to 1:100
1:20	80%	60%	40%	20%

change from	to 1:20	to 1:33	to 1:50	to 1:100
1:25	125%	75%	50%	25%

change from	to 1:20	to 1:25	to 1:50	to 1:100
1:33	167%	133%	67%	33%

change from	to 1:20	to 1:25	to 1:33	to 1:100
1:50	200% + 125%	200%	150%	50%

change from	to 1:20	to 1:25	to 1:33	to 1:50
1:100	n/a	200% + 200%	200% + 150%	200%

Note: Photocopiers should never be used when accuracy is required, as they can be inaccurate.

131

measurement conversion tables
▤modelrooms

feet	metres*
1'	0.3 m
2'	0.6 m
3'	0.9 m
4'	1.2 m
5'	1.5 m
6'	1.8 m
7'	2.1 m
8'	2.4 m
9'	2.7 m
10'	3 m
11'	3.4 m
12'	3.7 m
13'	4 m
14'	4.3 m
15'	4.6 m
16'	4.9 m
17'	5.2 m
18'	5.5 m
19'	5.8 m
20'	6.1 m

*All metric measurements rounded to nearest 100mm

metres	feet*
1 m	3' 3"
1.25 m	4' 1"
1.5 m	4' 11"
1.75 m	5' 9"
2 m	6' 7"
2.25 m	7' 5"
2.5 m	8' 2"
2.75 m	9'
3 m	9' 10"
3.25 m	10' 8"
3.5 m	11' 6"
3.75 m	12' 4"
4 m	13' 1"
4.25 m	13' 11'
4.5 m	14' 9"
4.75 m	15' 7"
5 m	16' 5"
5.25 m	17' 3"
5.5 m	18' 1"
5.75 m	18' 10"
6 m	19' 8"

*All imperial measurements rounded to nearest inch

other ⬚model rooms products

Home Design Kit

Our Home Design Kits come with larger scale pieces (1:33), magnetic walls and windows, and two A4 solid baseboards. If you plan to extend or build then they are the perfect solution to help you quickly create scale plans using magnets.

Contents Include:

2 X A4 sized baseboards (up to 140m2)

80+ Kitchen furniture magnets

70+ living and Bedroom Magnets

50+ Bathroom furniture magnets

200+ Walls, window and door magnets

Metric and imperial scale rules

A4 Storage tin

Flash cards to help plan the perfect layout

Professional Design Kit

Our Premium Design Kit for the professional user.

Contents Include:

2 X A4 sized baseboards (up to 140m2)

80+ Kitchen furniture magnets

70+ living and Bedroom Magnets

50+ Bathroom furniture magnets

200+ Walls, window and door magnets

Metric and imperial scale rules

A4 Storage tin

Pack of flash cards

Home Office furniture magnets

Home Gym, jacuzzi & sauna furniture magnets

Home Entertainement &Gamesroom magnets

Garage magnets

Professional Scale rule with 3 additional scales

Portfolio Carry Case

Order Form

Online:

Go to our website products page to see our full range of products:

www.modelrooms.com

Phone:

Give us a call with credit/debit card details:
00353 (0)1 4539990 IRL / Intnl
08454565886   UK

Mail Order:

Send us a cheque/postal order with a copy of this page to:

Modelrooms, Unit 6, Sunshine Industrial Est, Crumlin Road, Dublin 12, Ireland

Product	IRL	UK	Qty	Total
Home Design Kit	€79	£49		
Professional Design Kit	€129	£79		
Postage per order (UK and IRL only)	€10	£7		
Total				

Method of Payment:

Cheque ☐   Postal order ☐   Credit Card ☐

Credit Card Details

Type _____   Expiry Date _____

Number ☐☐☐☐☐☐☐☐☐☐☐☐☐☐☐☐☐

Name (on card): _____

Delivery Address _____

_____

_____

Contact No: _____

Email: _____

kitchen magnets

images	item & dimensions(mm)	qty	image	item & dimensions(mm)	qty
	Rectangular dining tables 1500 x 1000 & 1200 x 800	2		American Fridge 900 x 600	1
	Circular dining table Diameter (d) 1200	1		Sinks 800 X 600	2
	Square Dining Tables 1000 x 1000 & 800 x 800	2		Drainingboard for Sink 600 x 400	2
	Dining Chair 500 x 430	8		Left & Right Handed Sinks 1000 x 600	2
	Kitchen Units 1000 x 600 & 800 x 600	3		Round Sink 600 x 600	1
	Kitchen Units 600 x 600 & 600 x 500	15		Tumble Dryer 600 x 600	1
	Kitchen Units 600 x 400 & 600 x 300			Dishwasher 600 x 600	1
	Counter Top Items 600 x 600	2		Island Unit 1500 x 1000	1
	Counter Top Items 600 x 600	2		Washing Machine 600 x 600	1
	Cooker Hobs 600 x 600 & 600 x 300	2		Top Loader 600 x 600	1
	Large Cooker 900 x 600	1		Wine Rack Cabinet 600 x 300	2
	Fridges 600 x 600	2		Rounded End Units d+1000 & d=800	4

Please note: Images for illustration purposes only, not to scale. All measurements rounded to nearest 50mm and based on standard sizes.

bathroom magnets

images	item & dimensions(mm)	qty	image	item & dimensions(mm)	qty
	Corner Bath 1200 x 1200	1		Small Toilet 750 x 450	1
	Small Bath 1500 x 650	1		Regular Toilet 800 x 550	1
	Standard Bath 1700 x 750	1		Corner Toilet 650 x 650	1
	Freestanding Bath 1700 x 900	1		Small Corner Sink 500 x 500	1
	Shower-Bath Left 1700 x 900	1		Large Corner Sink 600 x 600	1
	Shower-Bath Right 1700 x 900	1		Small Sink 600 x 350	1
	Corner Shower 900 x 900	1		Large Sink 850 x 400	1
	LHand Corner Shower 1550 x x1000	1		Double Sink 1000 x 500	1
	RHand Corner Shower 1550 x x1000	1		Round Sink Unit 900 x 500	1
	Square Shower 800 x 800	1		Storage Unit 500 x 500	3
	Square Shower 900 x 900	1		Storage Unit 400 x 400	2
	Rectangular Shower 1250 x 850	1		Laundry Unit 400 x 400	1

Please note: Images for illustration purposes only, not to scale. All measurements rounded to nearest 50mm and based on standard sizes.

living and bedroom magnets

images	item & dimensions(mm)	qty	image	item & dimensions(mm)	qty
	Corner Sofa Unit 800 x 800	6		Shelving Unit 750 x 300	2
	Sofa Unit 800 x 500	6		Sideboard 800 x 400	1
	Sofa Chair 1000 x 800	2		Televisions 1000 x 500 & 1000 x 300	2
	Tub Chair 800 x 800	2		Fireplaces 1200 x 350 & 750 x 250	2
	Coffee Tables 1000x600, 1000x500 & d=450	3		Long Media Table 1000 x 500	1
	Super Kingsize/Kingsize Bed* 2000 x 1800	1		Double Bed 1900 x 1350	2
	Single Bed 1900 x 1000	2		Bedside Lockers 500 x 500	6
	Dresser 500 x 500	6		Wardrobe 500 x 500	12

additional pieces

	Stardard Internal Door 800 (width)	8		Straight Staircase 1300 x 1000	1
	1:50 scale rule	1		Corner Staircase 1400 x 1400 (stair width 1000)	1
	Wheelchair Turning Circle d=1500	1		Spiral Staircase d=1600 (stair width 750)	1

Please note: Images for illustration purposes only, not to scale. All measurements rounded to nearest 50mm and based on standard sizes.

*Note: We have found that some furniture retailers refer to this size bed as King size and others as Super king. Always check dimensions.

1:50 grid

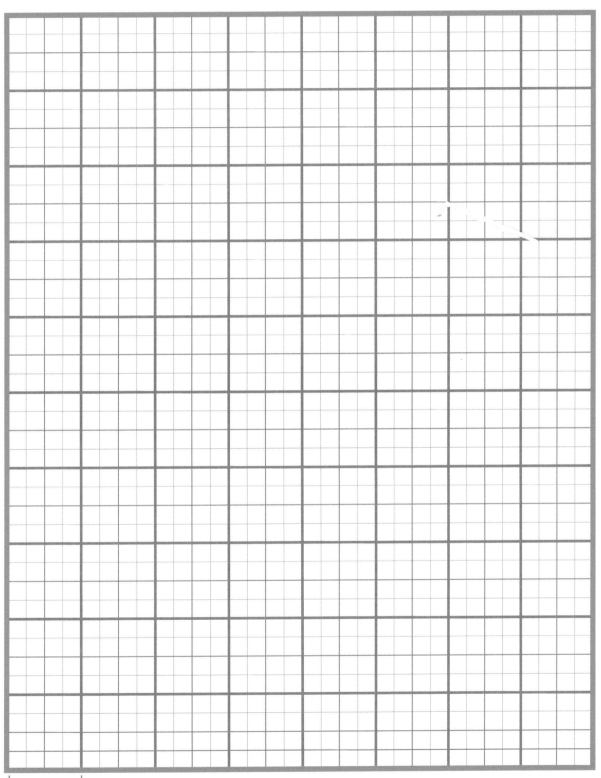

1m at 1:50

1:50 grid

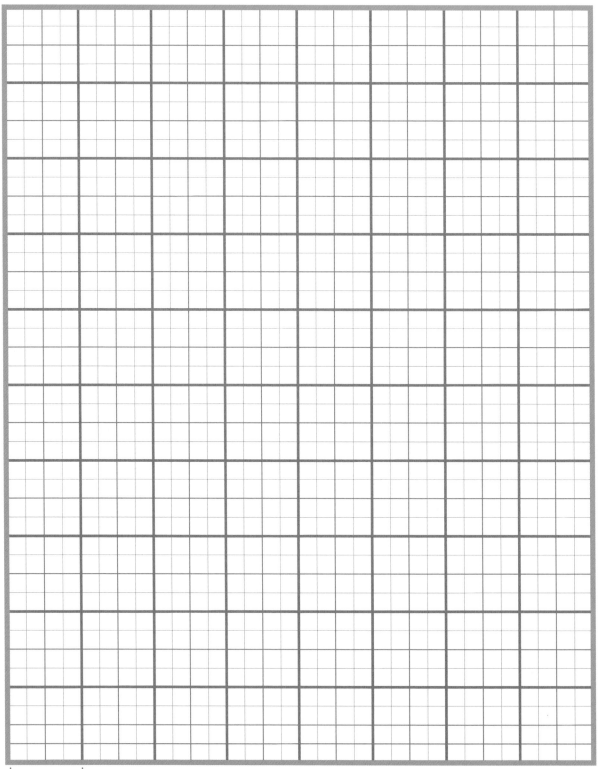

1m at 1:50

1-5pm Sat 9am-1pm

Page 44

revealed inside

1:50 grid

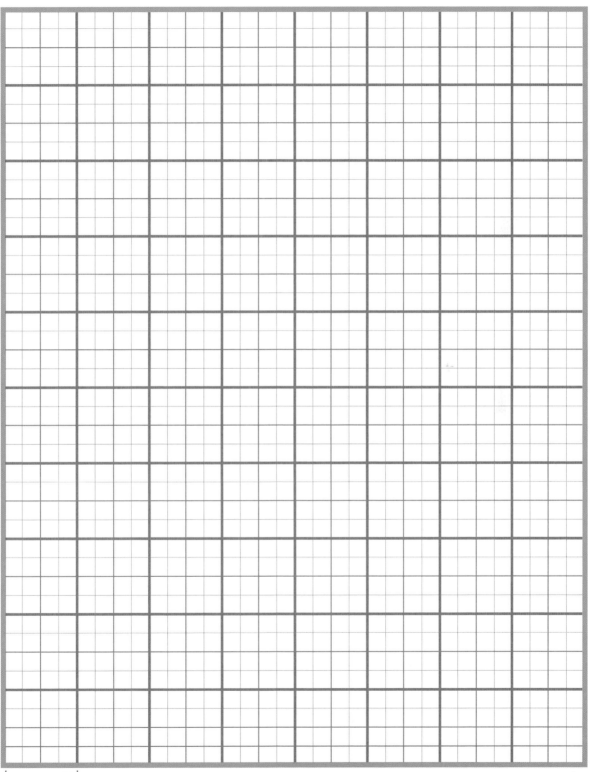

1m at 1:50

1:50 grid

modelrooms

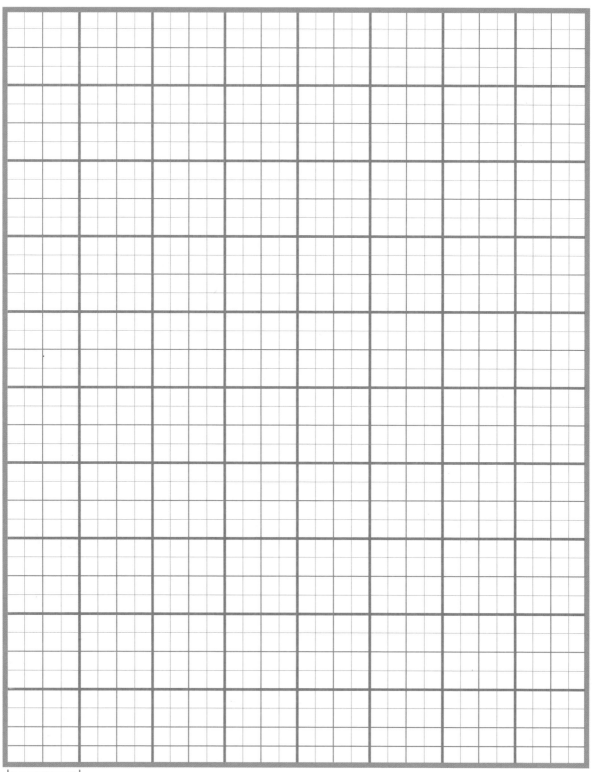

1m at 1:50